w

50 Seafood Sensation Recipes for Home

By: Kelly Johnson

Table of Contents

- Garlic Butter Shrimp
- Lemon Herb Grilled Salmon
- Spicy Tuna Tartare
- Baked Cod with Tomatoes and Olives
- Creamy Lobster Pasta
- Blackened Mahi-Mahi Tacos
- Seafood Paella
- Shrimp Scampi
- Clam Chowder
- Honey Soy Glazed Salmon
- Fish and Chips
- Grilled Octopus Salad
- Shrimp and Grits
- Crab Cakes with Remoulade
- Seared Scallops with Lemon Beurre Blanc
- Fish Tacos with Cabbage Slaw
- Spaghetti Vongole (Clam Pasta)
- Thai Coconut Curry Shrimp
- Baked Stuffed Lobster
- Fish en Papillote
- Shrimp Ceviche
- Pesto Grilled Shrimp Skewers
- Szechuan Peppercorn Salmon
- Miso Glazed Black Cod
- Bouillabaisse
- Fish Chowder with Corn
- Coconut Shrimp with Mango Salsa
- Grilled Sardines with Lemon
- Shrimp Fried Rice
- Clams Casino
- Crab and Avocado Salad
- Lobster Bisque
- Teriyaki Salmon Bowls
- Mussels in White Wine Sauce
- Fish Curry with Coconut Milk

- Cajun Shrimp Pasta
- Grilled Fish with Mango Salsa
- Sea Bass with Tomato Basil Salsa
- Thai Shrimp Soup (Tom Yum)
- Zucchini Noodles with Prawns
- Saffron Risotto with Scallops
- Baked Parmesan Crusted Tilapia
- Shrimp and Avocado Toast
- Oven-Roasted Whole Fish
- Fish Tikka Masala
- Crab Stuffed Bell Peppers
- Grilled Shrimp Caesar Salad
- Smoked Salmon Bagels
- Scallop and Bacon Skewers
- Shrimp and Corn Fritters

Garlic Butter Shrimp

Ingredients:

- 1 lb large shrimp, peeled and deveined
- 4 tablespoons butter
- 4 cloves garlic, minced
- 1/4 teaspoon red pepper flakes
- Salt and pepper (to taste)
- Fresh parsley, chopped (for garnish)

Instructions:

1. **Melt Butter**: In a large skillet over medium heat, melt butter.
2. **Sauté Garlic**: Add garlic and red pepper flakes, cooking for about 1 minute until fragrant.
3. **Cook Shrimp**: Add shrimp, season with salt and pepper, and cook for 3-4 minutes until pink and opaque.
4. **Serve**: Garnish with fresh parsley and serve warm.

Lemon Herb Grilled Salmon

Ingredients:

- 4 salmon fillets
- 2 tablespoons olive oil
- 2 tablespoons lemon juice
- 2 teaspoons dried oregano
- Salt and pepper (to taste)
- Lemon wedges (for serving)

Instructions:

1. **Prepare Marinade**: In a bowl, whisk together olive oil, lemon juice, oregano, salt, and pepper.
2. **Marinate Salmon**: Place salmon fillets in the marinade and let sit for 15-30 minutes.
3. **Preheat Grill**: Heat grill to medium-high.
4. **Grill Salmon**: Grill salmon for 5-6 minutes per side, or until cooked through.
5. **Serve**: Serve with lemon wedges.

Spicy Tuna Tartare

Ingredients:

- 1 lb sushi-grade tuna, diced
- 2 tablespoons soy sauce
- 1 tablespoon sesame oil
- 1 tablespoon Sriracha (adjust to taste)
- 1 tablespoon green onions, chopped
- Wonton chips (for serving)

Instructions:

1. **Mix Tuna**: In a bowl, combine diced tuna, soy sauce, sesame oil, Sriracha, and green onions. Mix gently.
2. **Chill**: Let the mixture chill in the refrigerator for 15 minutes.
3. **Serve**: Spoon tuna tartare onto wonton chips and enjoy.

Baked Cod with Tomatoes and Olives

Ingredients:

- 4 cod fillets
- 1 cup cherry tomatoes, halved
- 1/2 cup olives, sliced (kalamata or green)
- 3 tablespoons olive oil
- 2 cloves garlic, minced
- Salt and pepper (to taste)
- Fresh basil (for garnish)

Instructions:

1. **Preheat the Oven**: Preheat to 400°F (200°C).
2. **Prepare Baking Dish**: In a baking dish, place cod fillets and top with cherry tomatoes, olives, garlic, olive oil, salt, and pepper.
3. **Bake**: Bake for 15-20 minutes until fish is flaky and cooked through.
4. **Serve**: Garnish with fresh basil and serve.

Creamy Lobster Pasta

Ingredients:

- 8 oz fettuccine or linguine
- 1 cup cooked lobster meat, chopped
- 1 cup heavy cream
- 2 tablespoons butter
- 2 cloves garlic, minced
- 1/4 cup grated Parmesan cheese
- Salt and pepper (to taste)
- Fresh parsley (for garnish)

Instructions:

1. **Cook Pasta**: Cook pasta according to package instructions. Drain and set aside.
2. **Make Sauce**: In a skillet, melt butter and sauté garlic until fragrant. Add heavy cream and simmer for 5 minutes.
3. **Combine**: Stir in lobster meat, Parmesan, salt, and pepper. Add pasta and toss to combine.
4. **Serve**: Garnish with parsley and enjoy!

Blackened Mahi-Mahi Tacos

Ingredients:

- 2 Mahi-Mahi fillets
- 2 tablespoons blackening seasoning
- 8 small tortillas
- 1 cup cabbage, shredded
- Lime wedges (for serving)
- Avocado slices (optional)

Instructions:

1. **Season Fish**: Rub Mahi-Mahi fillets with blackening seasoning.
2. **Cook Fish**: Heat a skillet over high heat and cook fish for about 3-4 minutes per side until cooked through.
3. **Assemble Tacos**: Flake fish and place in tortillas. Top with cabbage and avocado.
4. **Serve**: Squeeze lime juice over tacos and enjoy!

Seafood Paella

Ingredients:

- 1 cup Arborio rice
- 2 cups seafood broth
- 1/2 lb shrimp, peeled and deveined
- 1/2 lb mussels, cleaned
- 1/2 lb squid, sliced
- 1/2 cup peas
- 1 bell pepper, diced
- 1 onion, chopped
- 2 cloves garlic, minced
- 1 teaspoon smoked paprika
- Olive oil (for cooking)
- Fresh parsley (for garnish)

Instructions:

1. **Sauté Vegetables**: In a large skillet, heat olive oil and sauté onion, garlic, and bell pepper until soft.
2. **Add Rice**: Stir in Arborio rice and smoked paprika, cooking for 1-2 minutes.
3. **Add Broth**: Pour in seafood broth and bring to a simmer. Cook for about 15 minutes.
4. **Add Seafood**: Stir in shrimp, mussels, squid, and peas. Cover and cook until seafood is cooked through and rice is tender, about 5-7 minutes.
5. **Serve**: Garnish with parsley and enjoy!

Shrimp Scampi

Ingredients:

- 1 lb large shrimp, peeled and deveined
- 4 tablespoons butter
- 4 cloves garlic, minced
- 1/4 teaspoon red pepper flakes
- 1/4 cup white wine
- 1 lemon, juiced
- 1/4 cup fresh parsley, chopped
- Cooked pasta (for serving)

Instructions:

1. **Sauté Shrimp**: In a large skillet, melt butter and sauté garlic and red pepper flakes until fragrant. Add shrimp and cook until pink, about 3-4 minutes.
2. **Add Wine and Lemon**: Pour in white wine and lemon juice, simmering for 2 minutes.
3. **Serve**: Toss with cooked pasta and garnish with parsley before serving.

Enjoy these delicious seafood dishes!

Clam Chowder

Ingredients:

- 4 slices bacon, diced
- 1 onion, chopped
- 2 celery stalks, chopped
- 2 cloves garlic, minced
- 3 cups diced potatoes
- 4 cups clam juice
- 1 cup heavy cream
- 2 cans (6.5 oz each) chopped clams, drained
- Salt and pepper (to taste)
- Fresh parsley, chopped (for garnish)

Instructions:

1. **Cook Bacon**: In a large pot, cook bacon over medium heat until crispy. Remove and set aside.
2. **Sauté Vegetables**: In the same pot, add onion, celery, and garlic. Sauté until softened.
3. **Add Potatoes**: Stir in diced potatoes and clam juice. Bring to a boil, then simmer until potatoes are tender, about 15 minutes.
4. **Finish Chowder**: Stir in heavy cream and chopped clams. Season with salt and pepper. Heat through.
5. **Serve**: Top with cooked bacon and fresh parsley before serving.

Honey Soy Glazed Salmon

Ingredients:

- 4 salmon fillets
- 1/4 cup soy sauce
- 1/4 cup honey
- 2 tablespoons rice vinegar
- 2 cloves garlic, minced
- 1 teaspoon fresh ginger, grated
- Sesame seeds (for garnish)
- Green onions, sliced (for garnish)

Instructions:

1. **Make Marinade**: In a bowl, whisk together soy sauce, honey, rice vinegar, garlic, and ginger.
2. **Marinate Salmon**: Place salmon in a shallow dish and pour marinade over it. Let sit for 15-30 minutes.
3. **Preheat Grill**: Heat grill to medium-high.
4. **Grill Salmon**: Grill salmon for 4-5 minutes on each side until cooked through and caramelized.
5. **Serve**: Garnish with sesame seeds and green onions before serving.

Fish and Chips

Ingredients:

- 1 lb white fish fillets (cod or haddock)
- 1 cup all-purpose flour, divided
- 1 cup beer (or sparkling water)
- 1 teaspoon baking powder
- Salt and pepper (to taste)
- Oil (for frying)
- Frozen French fries (for serving)
- Malt vinegar (for serving)

Instructions:

1. **Prepare Batter**: In a bowl, combine 1 cup flour, beer, baking powder, salt, and pepper until smooth.
2. **Heat Oil**: In a large pot, heat oil over medium-high heat.
3. **Dredge Fish**: Dredge fish fillets in the remaining flour, then dip in the batter. Carefully place in hot oil and fry until golden, about 4-5 minutes per side.
4. **Cook Fries**: Prepare French fries according to package instructions.
5. **Serve**: Plate fish and chips with malt vinegar on the side.

Grilled Octopus Salad

Ingredients:

- 1 lb octopus, cleaned
- 1/4 cup olive oil
- 2 cloves garlic, minced
- 1 lemon, juiced
- 1 teaspoon smoked paprika
- Mixed greens (for serving)
- Cherry tomatoes, halved (for serving)
- Fresh parsley, chopped (for garnish)

Instructions:

1. **Cook Octopus**: In a pot of boiling salted water, cook octopus for about 45 minutes until tender. Drain and let cool.
2. **Grill Octopus**: Preheat grill to medium-high. Cut octopus into tentacles, brush with olive oil, garlic, lemon juice, and paprika. Grill for 2-3 minutes per side.
3. **Prepare Salad**: On a platter, arrange mixed greens and cherry tomatoes.
4. **Serve**: Slice grilled octopus and place on the salad. Garnish with parsley.

Shrimp and Grits

Ingredients:

- 1 cup grits
- 4 cups water
- 1 lb shrimp, peeled and deveined
- 4 slices bacon, diced
- 2 cloves garlic, minced
- 1 teaspoon paprika
- 1/4 cup green onions, chopped
- Salt and pepper (to taste)
- 1/2 cup shredded cheddar cheese (optional)

Instructions:

1. **Cook Grits**: In a pot, bring water to a boil. Stir in grits, reduce heat, and simmer for about 20 minutes until thickened. Stir in cheese if desired.
2. **Cook Bacon**: In a skillet, cook bacon until crispy. Remove and set aside, leaving drippings.
3. **Cook Shrimp**: In the same skillet, add garlic and sauté for 1 minute. Add shrimp, paprika, salt, and pepper. Cook until shrimp are pink, about 3-4 minutes.
4. **Serve**: Spoon grits onto plates and top with shrimp and bacon. Garnish with green onions.

Crab Cakes with Remoulade

Ingredients:

- 1 lb lump crab meat
- 1/2 cup breadcrumbs
- 1/4 cup mayonnaise
- 1 tablespoon Dijon mustard
- 1 egg
- 1 tablespoon Worcestershire sauce
- Salt and pepper (to taste)
- Oil (for frying)

For Remoulade:

- 1/2 cup mayonnaise
- 1 tablespoon Dijon mustard
- 1 tablespoon capers, chopped
- 1 tablespoon lemon juice
- Hot sauce (to taste)

Instructions:

1. **Make Crab Cakes**: In a bowl, combine crab meat, breadcrumbs, mayonnaise, mustard, egg, Worcestershire sauce, salt, and pepper. Form into patties.
2. **Fry Crab Cakes**: Heat oil in a skillet over medium heat. Fry crab cakes for 4-5 minutes on each side until golden brown.
3. **Make Remoulade**: In a small bowl, mix all remoulade ingredients together.
4. **Serve**: Serve crab cakes with remoulade on the side.

Seared Scallops with Lemon Beurre Blanc

Ingredients:

- 1 lb sea scallops
- Salt and pepper (to taste)
- 2 tablespoons olive oil
- 1/4 cup white wine
- 1/4 cup heavy cream
- 1/2 cup butter, cold and cubed
- 1 lemon, juiced

Instructions:

1. **Season Scallops**: Pat scallops dry and season with salt and pepper.
2. **Sear Scallops**: In a skillet, heat olive oil over high heat. Sear scallops for about 2-3 minutes per side until golden brown. Remove and keep warm.
3. **Make Sauce**: In the same skillet, add white wine and lemon juice, reducing by half. Stir in cream, then whisk in cold butter until emulsified.
4. **Serve**: Plate scallops and drizzle with lemon beurre blanc.

Fish Tacos with Cabbage Slaw

Ingredients:

- 1 lb white fish fillets (tilapia or cod)
- 1 tablespoon taco seasoning
- 8 small tortillas
- 2 cups cabbage, shredded
- 1/4 cup mayonnaise
- 1 tablespoon lime juice
- Avocado slices (for serving)
- Fresh cilantro (for garnish)

Instructions:

1. **Cook Fish**: Season fish with taco seasoning. Cook in a skillet over medium heat for 3-4 minutes per side until cooked through. Flake into pieces.
2. **Make Slaw**: In a bowl, combine cabbage, mayonnaise, and lime juice. Mix well.
3. **Assemble Tacos**: Place fish in tortillas, top with cabbage slaw and avocado slices.
4. **Serve**: Garnish with fresh cilantro and enjoy!

Enjoy these delightful seafood dishes!

Spaghetti Vongole (Clam Pasta)

Ingredients:

- 12 oz spaghetti
- 2 lbs fresh clams, scrubbed
- 4 tablespoons olive oil
- 4 cloves garlic, minced
- 1/2 teaspoon red pepper flakes
- 1 cup white wine
- 1/4 cup fresh parsley, chopped
- Salt and pepper (to taste)
- Lemon wedges (for serving)

Instructions:

1. **Cook Pasta**: Boil spaghetti according to package instructions. Reserve 1 cup pasta water, then drain.
2. **Sauté Garlic**: In a large skillet, heat olive oil over medium heat. Add garlic and red pepper flakes, sautéing for about 1 minute.
3. **Add Clams**: Pour in white wine and add clams. Cover and cook for 5-7 minutes until clams open.
4. **Combine**: Add cooked spaghetti and reserved pasta water to the skillet. Toss to combine, adding parsley, salt, and pepper.
5. **Serve**: Plate and serve with lemon wedges.

Thai Coconut Curry Shrimp

Ingredients:

- 1 lb shrimp, peeled and deveined
- 1 can (14 oz) coconut milk
- 2 tablespoons red curry paste
- 1 bell pepper, sliced
- 1 cup snap peas
- 2 tablespoons fish sauce
- 1 tablespoon lime juice
- Fresh cilantro (for garnish)
- Cooked rice (for serving)

Instructions:

1. **Sauté Curry Paste**: In a large skillet, heat coconut milk and red curry paste over medium heat, stirring until fragrant.
2. **Add Vegetables**: Add bell pepper and snap peas. Simmer for about 5 minutes until tender.
3. **Add Shrimp**: Stir in shrimp, fish sauce, and lime juice. Cook for 3-4 minutes until shrimp are pink and cooked through.
4. **Serve**: Serve over cooked rice and garnish with fresh cilantro.

Baked Stuffed Lobster

Ingredients:

- 2 whole lobsters, halved and cleaned
- 1 cup bread crumbs
- 1/4 cup melted butter
- 1/4 cup parsley, chopped
- 2 cloves garlic, minced
- Salt and pepper (to taste)
- 1/2 cup grated Parmesan cheese

Instructions:

1. **Preheat Oven**: Preheat to 375°F (190°C).
2. **Make Filling**: In a bowl, combine bread crumbs, melted butter, parsley, garlic, salt, pepper, and Parmesan.
3. **Stuff Lobsters**: Place lobster halves on a baking sheet and fill with stuffing mixture.
4. **Bake**: Bake for 15-20 minutes until lobster is cooked and topping is golden.
5. **Serve**: Enjoy warm.

Fish en Papillote

Ingredients:

- 2 fish fillets (such as sole or tilapia)
- 1 zucchini, thinly sliced
- 1 bell pepper, thinly sliced
- 1 lemon, sliced
- 2 tablespoons olive oil
- Salt and pepper (to taste)
- Fresh herbs (such as thyme or dill)

Instructions:

1. **Preheat Oven**: Preheat to 400°F (200°C).
2. **Prepare Parchment**: Cut two large pieces of parchment paper. Place vegetables in the center of each.
3. **Add Fish**: Place fish on top of vegetables. Drizzle with olive oil, season with salt and pepper, and top with lemon slices and herbs.
4. **Seal Pouches**: Fold parchment to create a sealed pouch, crimping the edges tightly.
5. **Bake**: Place on a baking sheet and bake for 15-20 minutes until fish is flaky.
6. **Serve**: Carefully open pouches and enjoy!

Shrimp Ceviche

Ingredients:

- 1 lb shrimp, peeled and deveined
- 1 cup lime juice (about 8 limes)
- 1/2 red onion, finely chopped
- 1 cucumber, diced
- 1 jalapeño, minced
- 1/4 cup cilantro, chopped
- Salt and pepper (to taste)

Instructions:

1. **Marinate Shrimp**: In a bowl, combine shrimp and lime juice. Let sit in the refrigerator for about 30 minutes until shrimp are opaque.
2. **Add Vegetables**: Drain excess lime juice and stir in red onion, cucumber, jalapeño, cilantro, salt, and pepper.
3. **Serve**: Serve chilled with tortilla chips.

Pesto Grilled Shrimp Skewers

Ingredients:

- 1 lb shrimp, peeled and deveined
- 1/2 cup pesto sauce
- 8 skewers (soaked in water if wooden)
- Cherry tomatoes (optional, for skewering)

Instructions:

1. **Marinate Shrimp**: In a bowl, combine shrimp and pesto. Let marinate for 15-30 minutes.
2. **Preheat Grill**: Heat grill to medium-high.
3. **Skewer Shrimp**: Thread shrimp (and cherry tomatoes, if using) onto skewers.
4. **Grill**: Grill skewers for about 2-3 minutes per side until shrimp are pink and cooked through.
5. **Serve**: Enjoy warm.

Szechuan Peppercorn Salmon

Ingredients:

- 4 salmon fillets
- 2 tablespoons Szechuan peppercorns, crushed
- 2 tablespoons soy sauce
- 1 tablespoon honey
- 1 teaspoon ginger, grated
- 1 tablespoon olive oil
- Green onions (for garnish)

Instructions:

1. **Make Marinade**: In a bowl, mix Szechuan peppercorns, soy sauce, honey, ginger, and olive oil.
2. **Marinate Salmon**: Place salmon fillets in the marinade for 15-30 minutes.
3. **Preheat Grill**: Heat grill to medium-high.
4. **Grill Salmon**: Grill salmon for 4-5 minutes on each side until cooked through.
5. **Serve**: Garnish with sliced green onions.

Miso Glazed Black Cod

Ingredients:

- 4 black cod fillets
- 1/2 cup miso paste
- 1/4 cup sake
- 1/4 cup mirin
- 2 tablespoons sugar
- Sesame seeds (for garnish)
- Green onions (for garnish)

Instructions:

1. **Make Marinade**: In a bowl, whisk together miso paste, sake, mirin, and sugar until smooth.
2. **Marinate Cod**: Place cod fillets in a dish and cover with marinade. Refrigerate for at least 4 hours or overnight.
3. **Preheat Oven**: Preheat to 400°F (200°C).
4. **Bake Cod**: Place cod on a baking sheet lined with parchment and bake for 15-20 minutes until cooked through and flaky.
5. **Serve**: Garnish with sesame seeds and green onions.

Enjoy these exquisite seafood dishes!

Bouillabaisse

Ingredients:

- 2 tablespoons olive oil
- 1 onion, chopped
- 2 leeks, sliced
- 2 cloves garlic, minced
- 1 can (14 oz) diced tomatoes
- 4 cups fish stock
- 1/2 teaspoon saffron threads
- 1 lb mixed seafood (such as shrimp, mussels, and white fish)
- 1/2 teaspoon red pepper flakes
- Salt and pepper (to taste)
- Fresh parsley, chopped (for garnish)
- Crusty bread (for serving)

Instructions:

1. **Sauté Vegetables**: In a large pot, heat olive oil over medium heat. Add onion, leeks, and garlic; sauté until softened.
2. **Add Stock and Tomatoes**: Stir in diced tomatoes, fish stock, saffron, and red pepper flakes. Bring to a simmer.
3. **Add Seafood**: Add mixed seafood and cook for about 5-7 minutes until seafood is cooked through.
4. **Serve**: Season with salt and pepper, garnish with parsley, and serve with crusty bread.

Fish Chowder with Corn

Ingredients:

- 4 slices bacon, diced
- 1 onion, chopped
- 2 cloves garlic, minced
- 2 cups potatoes, diced
- 2 cups corn (fresh or frozen)
- 4 cups fish stock
- 1 cup heavy cream
- 1 lb white fish (such as cod), cut into bite-sized pieces
- Salt and pepper (to taste)
- Fresh thyme (for garnish)

Instructions:

1. **Cook Bacon**: In a large pot, cook bacon over medium heat until crispy. Remove and set aside.
2. **Sauté Vegetables**: In the bacon drippings, add onion and garlic, cooking until softened.
3. **Add Potatoes and Stock**: Stir in potatoes, corn, and fish stock. Bring to a boil, then simmer until potatoes are tender.
4. **Finish Chowder**: Stir in cream and fish. Cook until fish is cooked through, about 5 minutes.
5. **Serve**: Garnish with thyme and crispy bacon before serving.

Coconut Shrimp with Mango Salsa

Ingredients:

- 1 lb large shrimp, peeled and deveined
- 1 cup shredded coconut
- 1/2 cup flour
- 2 eggs, beaten
- Oil (for frying)

For Mango Salsa:

- 1 ripe mango, diced
- 1/2 red onion, finely chopped
- 1 jalapeño, minced
- Juice of 1 lime
- Fresh cilantro, chopped
- Salt (to taste)

Instructions:

1. **Prepare Salsa**: In a bowl, combine mango, red onion, jalapeño, lime juice, cilantro, and salt. Set aside.
2. **Batter Shrimp**: Dredge shrimp in flour, dip in beaten eggs, then coat with shredded coconut.
3. **Fry Shrimp**: Heat oil in a skillet over medium-high heat. Fry shrimp until golden brown, about 2-3 minutes per side.
4. **Serve**: Serve shrimp with mango salsa on the side.

Grilled Sardines with Lemon

Ingredients:

- 1 lb fresh sardines, cleaned
- 2 tablespoons olive oil
- Salt and pepper (to taste)
- Lemon wedges (for serving)
- Fresh parsley, chopped (for garnish)

Instructions:

1. **Prepare Sardines**: Rinse sardines and pat dry. Drizzle with olive oil, and season with salt and pepper.
2. **Preheat Grill**: Heat grill to medium-high.
3. **Grill Sardines**: Grill sardines for about 3-4 minutes per side until cooked through and charred.
4. **Serve**: Garnish with parsley and serve with lemon wedges.

Shrimp Fried Rice

Ingredients:

- 1 lb shrimp, peeled and deveined
- 3 cups cooked rice (preferably day-old)
- 2 tablespoons soy sauce
- 2 eggs, beaten
- 1 cup mixed vegetables (peas, carrots, corn)
- 2 cloves garlic, minced
- 2 green onions, chopped
- Oil (for cooking)

Instructions:

1. **Cook Shrimp**: In a large skillet or wok, heat oil over medium-high heat. Add shrimp and cook until pink. Remove and set aside.
2. **Scramble Eggs**: In the same skillet, add more oil and scramble the beaten eggs. Remove and set aside.
3. **Sauté Vegetables**: Add garlic and mixed vegetables to the skillet, cooking until tender.
4. **Combine**: Stir in cooked rice, soy sauce, shrimp, and scrambled eggs. Toss to combine and heat through.
5. **Serve**: Garnish with green onions before serving.

Clams Casino

Ingredients:

- 12 large clams, shucked
- 4 slices bacon, cooked and crumbled
- 1/2 cup breadcrumbs
- 1/4 cup bell pepper, finely chopped
- 1/4 cup green onions, chopped
- 2 tablespoons parsley, chopped
- 1 tablespoon lemon juice
- 1 teaspoon Worcestershire sauce
- Olive oil (for drizzling)

Instructions:

1. **Preheat Oven**: Preheat to 400°F (200°C).
2. **Make Topping**: In a bowl, mix breadcrumbs, crumbled bacon, bell pepper, green onions, parsley, lemon juice, and Worcestershire sauce.
3. **Fill Clams**: Place shucked clams on a baking sheet. Spoon topping mixture over each clam.
4. **Bake**: Drizzle with olive oil and bake for 10-15 minutes until golden and heated through.
5. **Serve**: Enjoy warm.

Crab and Avocado Salad

Ingredients:

- 1 lb lump crab meat
- 2 ripe avocados, diced
- 1/2 red onion, finely chopped
- 1/4 cup cilantro, chopped
- Juice of 1 lime
- Salt and pepper (to taste)

Instructions:

1. **Combine Ingredients**: In a bowl, gently mix crab meat, avocados, red onion, cilantro, lime juice, salt, and pepper.
2. **Serve**: Serve chilled on its own or with crackers.

Lobster Bisque

Ingredients:

- 2 lobsters (about 1 lb each), cooked and shells reserved
- 4 tablespoons butter
- 1 onion, chopped
- 2 cloves garlic, minced
- 1 carrot, diced
- 1 celery stalk, diced
- 1 cup tomato puree
- 4 cups seafood stock
- 1 cup heavy cream
- 1/4 cup brandy
- Salt and pepper (to taste)
- Fresh chives (for garnish)

Instructions:

1. **Sauté Vegetables**: In a large pot, melt butter and sauté onion, garlic, carrot, and celery until softened.
2. **Add Stock and Puree**: Stir in tomato puree and seafood stock. Bring to a simmer.
3. **Add Lobster**: Remove meat from lobster shells and chop. Add lobster meat and shells to the pot, along with brandy. Simmer for 20 minutes.
4. **Blend Soup**: Remove shells and use an immersion blender to puree the soup until smooth.
5. **Finish Bisque**: Stir in heavy cream and season with salt and pepper. Heat through and serve garnished with chives.

Enjoy these delectable seafood dishes!

Teriyaki Salmon Bowls

Ingredients:

- 4 salmon fillets
- 1/2 cup teriyaki sauce
- 2 cups cooked rice (brown or white)
- 1 cup steamed broccoli
- 1 cup shredded carrots
- 1 avocado, sliced
- Sesame seeds (for garnish)
- Green onions, chopped (for garnish)

Instructions:

1. **Marinate Salmon**: In a bowl, marinate salmon fillets in teriyaki sauce for at least 30 minutes.
2. **Cook Salmon**: Preheat grill or skillet to medium-high heat. Cook salmon for about 4-5 minutes per side until cooked through.
3. **Assemble Bowls**: In bowls, layer cooked rice, steamed broccoli, shredded carrots, and sliced avocado. Top with salmon.
4. **Garnish**: Sprinkle with sesame seeds and green onions before serving.

Mussels in White Wine Sauce

Ingredients:

- 2 lbs mussels, cleaned
- 2 tablespoons olive oil
- 4 cloves garlic, minced
- 1 cup white wine
- 1/2 cup heavy cream
- 1/4 cup parsley, chopped
- Salt and pepper (to taste)
- Crusty bread (for serving)

Instructions:

1. **Sauté Garlic**: In a large pot, heat olive oil over medium heat. Add garlic and sauté for 1 minute.
2. **Add Wine**: Pour in white wine and bring to a simmer. Add mussels and cover the pot.
3. **Cook Mussels**: Cook for about 5-7 minutes until mussels open.
4. **Finish Sauce**: Stir in heavy cream and parsley. Season with salt and pepper.
5. **Serve**: Serve mussels with sauce and crusty bread.

Fish Curry with Coconut Milk

Ingredients:

- 1 lb white fish fillets (like cod)
- 2 tablespoons coconut oil
- 1 onion, chopped
- 2 cloves garlic, minced
- 1 tablespoon ginger, grated
- 2 tablespoons curry powder
- 1 can (14 oz) coconut milk
- 1 cup diced tomatoes
- 1 cup spinach
- Fresh cilantro (for garnish)
- Cooked rice (for serving)

Instructions:

1. **Sauté Onion**: In a large skillet, heat coconut oil over medium heat. Add onion, garlic, and ginger; sauté until softened.
2. **Add Spices**: Stir in curry powder and cook for another minute.
3. **Add Coconut Milk**: Pour in coconut milk and diced tomatoes. Bring to a simmer.
4. **Cook Fish**: Add fish fillets and cook for about 5-7 minutes until fish is cooked through. Stir in spinach until wilted.
5. **Serve**: Garnish with cilantro and serve over cooked rice.

Cajun Shrimp Pasta

Ingredients:

- 1 lb shrimp, peeled and deveined
- 8 oz fettuccine or pasta of choice
- 2 tablespoons Cajun seasoning
- 2 tablespoons olive oil
- 1 bell pepper, sliced
- 1 onion, chopped
- 2 cloves garlic, minced
- 1 cup heavy cream
- Parmesan cheese (for serving)

Instructions:

1. **Cook Pasta**: Cook pasta according to package instructions. Drain and set aside.
2. **Season Shrimp**: Toss shrimp with Cajun seasoning.
3. **Sauté Vegetables**: In a large skillet, heat olive oil over medium heat. Add bell pepper, onion, and garlic; sauté until softened.
4. **Cook Shrimp**: Add shrimp and cook until pink, about 3-4 minutes. Stir in heavy cream and heat through.
5. **Combine**: Toss pasta with shrimp and sauce. Serve with Parmesan cheese.

Grilled Fish with Mango Salsa

Ingredients:

- 4 fish fillets (such as tilapia or snapper)
- 2 tablespoons olive oil
- Salt and pepper (to taste)
- Juice of 1 lime

For Mango Salsa:

- 1 ripe mango, diced
- 1/2 red onion, finely chopped
- 1 jalapeño, minced
- Juice of 1 lime
- Fresh cilantro, chopped
- Salt (to taste)

Instructions:

1. **Make Salsa**: In a bowl, combine mango, red onion, jalapeño, lime juice, cilantro, and salt. Set aside.
2. **Season Fish**: Brush fish fillets with olive oil and season with salt, pepper, and lime juice.
3. **Grill Fish**: Preheat grill to medium-high. Grill fish for about 4-5 minutes per side until cooked through.
4. **Serve**: Top grilled fish with mango salsa.

Sea Bass with Tomato Basil Salsa

Ingredients:

- 4 sea bass fillets
- 2 tablespoons olive oil
- Salt and pepper (to taste)

For Tomato Basil Salsa:

- 2 cups cherry tomatoes, halved
- 1/4 cup fresh basil, chopped
- 1 tablespoon balsamic vinegar
- 1 tablespoon olive oil
- Salt and pepper (to taste)

Instructions:

1. **Make Salsa**: In a bowl, combine cherry tomatoes, basil, balsamic vinegar, olive oil, salt, and pepper. Set aside.
2. **Season Fish**: Brush sea bass fillets with olive oil and season with salt and pepper.
3. **Cook Fish**: Heat a skillet over medium-high heat and cook fish for about 4-5 minutes per side until flaky.
4. **Serve**: Top with tomato basil salsa.

Thai Shrimp Soup (Tom Yum)

Ingredients:

- 1 lb shrimp, peeled and deveined
- 4 cups chicken or vegetable broth
- 1 stalk lemongrass, sliced
- 3-4 kaffir lime leaves
- 2-3 slices galangal or ginger
- 2-3 Thai bird chilies (or to taste)
- 1 cup mushrooms, sliced
- 1 tablespoon fish sauce
- Juice of 1 lime
- Fresh cilantro (for garnish)

Instructions:

1. **Make Broth**: In a pot, bring broth, lemongrass, lime leaves, galangal, and chilies to a simmer.
2. **Add Mushrooms**: Add mushrooms and cook for about 5 minutes.
3. **Add Shrimp**: Stir in shrimp and cook until pink and cooked through, about 3-4 minutes.
4. **Finish Soup**: Remove from heat, add fish sauce and lime juice.
5. **Serve**: Garnish with fresh cilantro before serving.

Zucchini Noodles with Prawns

Ingredients:

- 1 lb prawns, peeled and deveined
- 4 medium zucchinis, spiralized
- 3 tablespoons olive oil
- 2 cloves garlic, minced
- 1/4 teaspoon red pepper flakes
- Salt and pepper (to taste)
- Fresh basil (for garnish)

Instructions:

1. **Sauté Garlic**: In a skillet, heat olive oil over medium heat. Add garlic and red pepper flakes; sauté for 1 minute.
2. **Cook Prawns**: Add prawns and cook until pink, about 3-4 minutes. Season with salt and pepper.
3. **Add Zoodles**: Toss in spiralized zucchini and cook for another 2-3 minutes until just tender.
4. **Serve**: Garnish with fresh basil before serving.

Enjoy these delicious seafood dishes!

Saffron Risotto with Scallops

Ingredients:

- 1 cup Arborio rice
- 4 cups chicken or vegetable broth
- 1 small onion, chopped
- 2 cloves garlic, minced
- 1/2 cup white wine
- 1/4 teaspoon saffron threads
- 1 tablespoon olive oil
- 1 tablespoon butter
- 1 cup scallops
- Salt and pepper (to taste)
- Fresh parsley, chopped (for garnish)
- Grated Parmesan cheese (for serving)

Instructions:

1. **Heat Broth**: In a saucepan, keep the broth warm over low heat.
2. **Sauté Aromatics**: In a large skillet, heat olive oil over medium heat. Add onion and garlic, sauté until translucent.
3. **Add Rice**: Stir in Arborio rice, cooking for 1-2 minutes until slightly toasted.
4. **Deglaze with Wine**: Pour in white wine, stirring until absorbed.
5. **Add Broth**: Gradually add warm broth, one ladle at a time, stirring frequently until absorbed before adding more. Stir in saffron halfway through cooking.
6. **Cook Scallops**: In another skillet, heat butter over medium-high heat. Season scallops with salt and pepper, then sear for 2-3 minutes per side until golden.
7. **Combine and Serve**: Plate the risotto, top with scallops, and garnish with parsley and Parmesan.

Baked Parmesan Crusted Tilapia

Ingredients:

- 4 tilapia fillets
- 1/2 cup grated Parmesan cheese
- 1/2 cup breadcrumbs
- 2 tablespoons melted butter
- 1 teaspoon garlic powder
- Salt and pepper (to taste)
- Lemon wedges (for serving)

Instructions:

1. **Preheat Oven**: Preheat to 400°F (200°C).
2. **Make Topping**: In a bowl, combine Parmesan, breadcrumbs, melted butter, garlic powder, salt, and pepper.
3. **Prepare Fish**: Place tilapia fillets on a baking sheet lined with parchment. Spoon topping over each fillet.
4. **Bake**: Bake for 15-20 minutes until fish flakes easily with a fork and topping is golden.
5. **Serve**: Enjoy with lemon wedges.

Shrimp and Avocado Toast

Ingredients:

- 1 lb shrimp, peeled and deveined
- 1 avocado, mashed
- 1 tablespoon lime juice
- 1/2 teaspoon garlic powder
- Salt and pepper (to taste)
- 4 slices of bread (sourdough or whole grain)
- Fresh cilantro, chopped (for garnish)

Instructions:

1. **Cook Shrimp**: In a skillet, heat olive oil over medium heat. Season shrimp with garlic powder, salt, and pepper. Cook until pink, about 3-4 minutes.
2. **Prepare Toast**: Toast bread slices until golden.
3. **Assemble**: Spread mashed avocado on each slice, top with cooked shrimp, and garnish with cilantro.
4. **Serve**: Enjoy immediately!

Oven-Roasted Whole Fish

Ingredients:

- 1 whole fish (such as snapper or trout), cleaned and scaled
- 2 lemons, sliced
- Fresh herbs (such as thyme or parsley)
- 4 cloves garlic, halved
- Olive oil
- Salt and pepper (to taste)

Instructions:

1. **Preheat Oven**: Preheat to 400°F (200°C).
2. **Prepare Fish**: Place the fish on a baking sheet lined with parchment. Stuff the cavity with lemon slices, herbs, and garlic.
3. **Season**: Drizzle with olive oil and season with salt and pepper.
4. **Roast**: Bake for 20-25 minutes until fish flakes easily with a fork.
5. **Serve**: Serve with additional lemon slices.

Fish Tikka Masala

Ingredients:

- 1 lb white fish (like cod), cut into cubes
- 1/2 cup plain yogurt
- 2 tablespoons tikka masala spice blend
- 1 tablespoon lemon juice
- 1 onion, chopped
- 2 cloves garlic, minced
- 1 can (14 oz) coconut milk
- Fresh cilantro, chopped (for garnish)

Instructions:

1. **Marinate Fish**: In a bowl, combine yogurt, tikka masala, and lemon juice. Add fish cubes and marinate for at least 30 minutes.
2. **Sauté Onions**: In a skillet, sauté onion and garlic until softened.
3. **Cook Fish**: Add marinated fish to the skillet and cook until opaque, about 5-7 minutes.
4. **Add Coconut Milk**: Stir in coconut milk and simmer for another 5 minutes.
5. **Serve**: Garnish with cilantro and serve with rice or naan.

Crab Stuffed Bell Peppers

Ingredients:

- 4 bell peppers, halved and seeds removed
- 1 lb lump crab meat
- 1 cup cooked rice
- 1/2 cup breadcrumbs
- 1/4 cup cream cheese, softened
- 2 green onions, chopped
- 1 tablespoon lemon juice
- Salt and pepper (to taste)
- Olive oil

Instructions:

1. **Preheat Oven**: Preheat to 375°F (190°C).
2. **Prepare Filling**: In a bowl, mix crab meat, rice, breadcrumbs, cream cheese, green onions, lemon juice, salt, and pepper.
3. **Stuff Peppers**: Fill each bell pepper half with the crab mixture and place in a baking dish.
4. **Drizzle and Bake**: Drizzle with olive oil and bake for 25-30 minutes until peppers are tender.
5. **Serve**: Enjoy warm.

Grilled Shrimp Caesar Salad

Ingredients:

- 1 lb shrimp, peeled and deveined
- 1 head romaine lettuce, chopped
- 1/4 cup Caesar dressing
- 1/4 cup grated Parmesan cheese
- Croutons (for serving)
- Olive oil
- Salt and pepper (to taste)

Instructions:

1. **Marinate Shrimp**: Toss shrimp with olive oil, salt, and pepper.
2. **Grill Shrimp**: Preheat grill to medium-high and grill shrimp for about 3-4 minutes per side until cooked through.
3. **Assemble Salad**: In a large bowl, combine romaine, Caesar dressing, and Parmesan cheese. Toss to coat.
4. **Top and Serve**: Add grilled shrimp on top and serve with croutons.

Smoked Salmon Bagels

Ingredients:

- 4 bagels, halved and toasted
- 8 oz cream cheese, softened
- 8 oz smoked salmon
- 1/2 red onion, thinly sliced
- Capers (for garnish)
- Fresh dill (for garnish)
- Lemon wedges (for serving)

Instructions:

1. **Spread Cream Cheese**: Spread cream cheese evenly on each bagel half.
2. **Top with Salmon**: Layer smoked salmon on top.
3. **Add Toppings**: Add red onion slices, capers, and dill.
4. **Serve**: Serve with lemon wedges on the side.

Enjoy these delicious seafood dishes!

Scallop and Bacon Skewers

Ingredients:

- 1 lb large sea scallops, cleaned
- 8 slices bacon, cut in half
- 1 tablespoon olive oil
- Salt and pepper (to taste)
- Fresh parsley, chopped (for garnish)
- Lemon wedges (for serving)

Instructions:

1. **Preheat Grill**: Preheat your grill to medium-high heat.
2. **Wrap Scallops**: Take each scallop and wrap a half slice of bacon around it, securing with a skewer.
3. **Season**: Brush with olive oil and season with salt and pepper.
4. **Grill Skewers**: Place skewers on the grill and cook for about 2-3 minutes per side, until bacon is crispy and scallops are opaque.
5. **Serve**: Garnish with parsley and serve with lemon wedges.

Shrimp and Corn Fritters

Ingredients:

- 1 lb shrimp, peeled and deveined, chopped
- 1 cup corn (fresh or frozen)
- 1/2 cup all-purpose flour
- 1/4 cup cornmeal
- 1/4 cup green onions, chopped
- 1 egg, beaten
- 1/2 teaspoon paprika
- Salt and pepper (to taste)
- Oil (for frying)

Instructions:

1. **Mix Ingredients**: In a bowl, combine shrimp, corn, flour, cornmeal, green onions, egg, paprika, salt, and pepper.
2. **Heat Oil**: In a skillet, heat oil over medium heat.
3. **Fry Fritters**: Drop spoonfuls of the mixture into the skillet and flatten slightly. Cook for about 3-4 minutes on each side until golden brown.
4. **Drain and Serve**: Drain on paper towels and serve warm, optionally with a dipping sauce.

Enjoy these delicious seafood appetizers!

www.ingramcontent.com/pod-product-compliance
Lightning Source LLC
LaVergne TN
LVHW081503060526
838201LV00056BA/2901